Table of Conte

C000103408

Introduction

Lebanon may be the smallest country in the Middle East, but is it is pretty big on flavor! The cuisine takes inspiration from surrounding Mediterranean countries on the west and Arab countries on the east. If one word describes a Lebanese dining table, it would probably be "lively". Meals in Lebanon are generally a very social occasion with large families sitting down together to share a meal!

Apart from the people, Lebanese tables are also crowded in terms of the variety and number of dishes. Mezzes or appetizers are usually laid out for everyone to share. You can usually find dishes of all tastes to suit every palate out there! Whether you enjoy lighter more healthier food or are in the mood for a more flavorsome feast, prefer eating utensils or bread to scoop up food, there's sure to be something for everyone at a Lebanese table!

Appetizers

1. Hummus bil Lahm – Hummus with Lamb

This quick and delicious appetizer is a Lebanese favorite that comes topped with warm minced lamb, toasted pine nuts and a quick drizzle of olive oil. Serve with warm pita bread!

Total Time: 1h

Servings: 4

Ingredients:

Spiced Lamb

- 4 oz. ground lamb
- 1/4 brown onion, finely diced
- ½ tbsp. olive oil
- ¼ tsp cumin powder
- ¼ tsp coriander powder
- ¼ tsp paprika powder
- Pinch of cinnamon powder
- 1/8 tsp black pepper

- ½ tsp salt

Hummus

- 1 8 oz. tin chickpeas, drained
- 2 tbsp. water
- ½ clove garlic
- Juice of ½ a small lemon
- 1 tbsp. tahini
- 1 tbsp. extra virgin olive oil
- Salt and pepper

Garnishes

- ½ tbsp. pine nuts
- Extra virgin olive oil

Instructions:

1. In a small pan over med-high heat, toast the pine nuts until nice and golden. Set aside.

2. Add olive oil and cook the onion for about 2 minutes until it turns translucent.

3. Increase heat to high and add the meat. Sprinkle on the spices and season. As the lamb cooks, break up the chunks into small pieces. Cook for 3 minutes.

4. Set the lamb aside to cool, covering the mixture so it doesn't dry out.

5. To make the hummus, add all the ingredients except the salt into a blender and process till smooth.

6. Season with salt and pepper as needed.

7. Add in some lemon juice if needed.

8. Adjust thickness with a little water. You want the consistency of a paste but not too thick.

9. Spread the hummus on a serving plate and top with the lamb mince. Sprinkle on the pine nuts and lightly drizzle with olive oil.

10. Serve with pita bread.

2. Kibbeh – Crunchy meatballs

Kibbeh is a popular appetizer in Lebanon. With a crunchy coating that holds delicious meat filling inside, these kibbehs are best served warm with a little tahini sauce.

Total Time: 2h 15m

Servings: 12-15 kibbehs

Ingredients:

Dough

- 1 ¼ cup fine bulgur wheat
- Water
- ½ large onion, quartered
- 12 oz. lean ground beef (or lamb)
- 1 tsp ground allspice
- ½ tsp ground coriander
- ¼ tsp ground cinnamon
- ½ tsp black pepper

- Pinch salt
- Oil for frying

Meat Filling

- Olive oil
- ½ medium yellow onion, finely chopped or grated
- 8 oz. ground lamb or beef (I used beef here), cold
- ¼ cup toasted pine nuts
- ½ tsp ground allspice
- ¼ tsp ground cinnamon
- Pinch salt and pepper

Instructions:

1. Start by soaking the wheat in water for 15 minutes. Then grab a light cloth (or a cheesecloth) and place it into a fine strainer. Drain the wheat into the cloth and squeeze to remove excess water. Set aside.

2. Add the rest of the dough ingredients into a food processor and process till fine – almost like a paste.

3. Combine the meat mixture with the wheat in a large bowl. Use your hands to ensure even mixing. Cover and chill for later.

4. To make the filling, heat ½ a tbsp. of olive oil in a pan. Add in the onions and sauté until brown. Add in the ground beef or lamb. Stir occasionally while cooking on medium heat until meat has cooked through. Add in the toasted nuts and the spices. Season according to taste and set aside to cool.

5. Line a baking sheet with baking paper.

6. Once the filling mixture cools, begin assembling the kibbeh. To do this, you'll need to consistently wet your hands. It is recommended to keep a bowl of water nearby.

7. With damp hands, take up about 2 tbsp. of dough mixture and form an oval shaped disc. Using your finger, create a well in the center. This is where the filling will go. Fill with about 1 tbsp. of filling and pinch the dough closed to form a football shape.

8. Place the kibbeh onto your baking sheet and repeat with the rest of the dough. Ensure your hands are damp throughout.

9. Chill for about 1 hour before frying.

10. To cook the kibbeh, heat oil in a large frying pan. The oil should be hot enough with slight bubbling on top – about 350 F.

11. Carefully deep fry the kibbeh in batches if necessary so as not to overcrowd the pan. Fry until brown – about 5 minutes.

12. Remove from oil and place on paper towel lined tray to drain.

13. Serve with tahini sauce and enjoy!

NOTES

Keeping the dough cool is pretty important while making the kibbehs. If you think you are going to take long to make them, keep the dough bowl in a larger bowl filled with ice.

These kibbehs can also be baked. Preheat oven to 400 F. Spray the formed kibbehs with olive oil and bake for about 30 minutes. Turn halfway to bake evenly.

3. Muhammara – Pepper and walnut spread

This flavorful spread is a great addition at any gathering. The spicy bite from the cayenne pepper combined with the sweet flavor of the roasted red bell pepper are both a joy for the taste buds!

Total Time: 45m

Serves: 8

Ingredients:

- ½ cup coarsely chopped roasted red bell pepper (drained), store-bought or prepared fresh
- ¼ cup finely chopped yellow onion
- 2 cups finely ground walnuts
- ½ cup seasoned bread crumbs
- ½ tsp cayenne pepper
- 2 tsp ground cumin
- 2 tsp ground paprika

- 1 tsp salt
- 2 tbsp. pomegranate molasses
- ¼ cup tomato paste
- ½ cup extra-virgin olive oi

Instructions:

1. Cut red bell peppers in half. Remove the ribs and seeds. Place the halves on a foil-lined baking sheet skin-side up. Place in the oven under the broiler set on high and broil until the skins blister. Remove the tray. Cover the peppers allowing them to steam for a few minutes. Peel and discard the blistered skins.

2. Place the bell pepper and onion in a food processor fitted with a metal blade and process to a pulp. Scrape down the sides with a spatula a couple of times. Add the remaining ingredients and pulse several times until well combined. The spread should retain the texture of ground walnuts, with a paste like consistency. Refrigerate for at least 2 hours prior to serving.

3. To serve, spread over a flat serving dish and smooth out the top. Use the rounded top of the back of a spoon to make indentations in the spread. Garnish with chopped walnuts and enjoy!

4. Sfiha Lahm – Meat pies

These pies are great as an afternoon snack or as an appetizer. The crisp texture of the edges balance out the savory flavors of the topping, while the addition of the pomegranate molasses lends a delicious sweet note to the dish!

Total Time: 1h 30m

Serves: 36 mini pies

Ingredients:

Dough –

- 1 cup plus 1 tbsp. lukewarm water
- 1½ tsp dry active yeast
- ¼ tsp sugar
- 3 cups unbleached all-purpose flour

- ¾ tsp salt
- 3 tbsp. extra-virgin olive oil
- 1/3 cup extra virgin olive oil for dipping

Topping –

- 1/3 cup toasted pine nuts
- ½ tbsp. melted butter
- 1 pound ground beef (80% lean)
- 3 cups diced yellow onion (¼ inch)
- 2½ tsp salt
- ½ tsp table-grind black pepper
- 1 tsp ground allspice
- ½ tsp ground cinnamon
- ¼ cup freshly squeezed lemon juice
- ½ cup cream cheese
- 2 tbsp. pomegranate molasses
- 1 tbsp. tahini (mix well before using)
- ½ cup pomegranate seeds

Instructions:

1. Preheat the oven to 350°F. Spread the pine nuts over a foil-lined baking sheet and toast in the center of the oven, shaking the pan occasionally, for 5 to 7 minutes or until the nuts are golden. Mix ½ tbsp. melted butter with the nuts. Transfer them to a paper towel–lined dish and set aside.

2. Preheat a large skillet over medium-high heat. Add the ground meat and cook while breaking it into small, minced pieces. Once the meat is no longer pink, add the onions, salt, pepper, allspice, and cinnamon. Reduce heat to medium-low and sauté, stirring periodically, until the onions are tender. Add the lemon juice and simmer until the moisture is absorbed.

3. Remove the skillet from the heat. Add the cheese, molasses, and tahini. Mix well and set aside until needed. Gently fold in the fresh pomegranate seeds.

4. Just before rolling the dough, preheat the oven to 450°F. Line a baking sheet with foil and set it within reach. Roll out half of the dough on a lightly floured surface to ¼ inch thickness. Cut the dough into 2-inch rounds using a cookie cutter; make one cut directly next to the other to maximize the amount

of rounds.

5. Do this with the rest of the dough. Using a pastry brush, coat each side of the dough with olive oil. Using your fingers, stretch out each piece of dough to 2 ½ inches by pressing down in the center and pushing to the edge.

6. Scoop 1 full tbsp. of topping into the center of each piece of dough. Use the tines of a fork to press and distribute the topping up to, but not over, the lip. Place 5 pine nuts on the meat topping of each pie and use the tines of the fork to gently press them into the topping.

7. Place the tray on the middle rack in the oven. Bake the pies for 10 to 12 minutes, or until the edges are a golden color. Cool slightly before serving.

5. Batata Harara – Spicy Potato Bites

This delicious potato dish is a great alternative to regular old potato salad and works wonderfully as an appetizer!

Total Time: 1h

Serves: 6 servings

Ingredients:

Potatoes -

- 2 lb. potatoes, peeled and cut into bite-sized pieces
- 1½ tbsp. olive oil
- ½ tsp. salt

Seasoning -

- 1 tbsp. olive oil
- 2 cloves garlic, minced
- ½ tsp. cumin
- ½ tsp. coriander

- ½ tsp. paprika
- ½ tsp. red chili powder
- ½ tsp. black pepper

Garnish -

- ¼ tsp. salt
- 3 tbsp. finely chopped cilantro
- 1 tsp lemon juice

Instructions:

1) Preheat oven to 450°F.

2) In a large bowl, combine the cut potatoes with the olive oil, and salt. Coat evenly.

3) Line a baking tray with parchment paper and roast the potatoes for 30-40 minutes or until golden brown. Remove from oven and set aside.

4) To make the seasoning, heat oil in a pan on medium. Add in the ginger and cook for about a minute. Remove from heat.

5) Immediately add in the remaining spices while the oil is still hot and mix thoroughly. Spread the seasoning mixture onto the potatoes and toss to combine evenly.

6) Sprinkle on the extra salt, cilantro, and lemon juice and toss again.

7) Serve warm!

6. Baba Ganoush – Smokey Eggplant Dip

Great-tasting baba ganoush has a subtle smoky flavor with just the right balance of lemon, tahini, and garlic. Offer it either as an appetizer, on a dinner buffet or take it along to barbecue night!

Total Time: 2h

Serves: 8

Ingredients:

- 2 large eggplants
- 3 tbsp. olive oil
- Juice of ½ lemon
- ½ cup Greek yogurt
- 2 cloves garlic

- Pinch of ground cumin
- Salt and pepper
- Chopped parsley for garnish

Instructions:

1) Preheat oven to 375 F.

2) Prick the skins of the eggplants with a fork and place on a baking sheet.

3) Bake eggplants for 45 minutes or until very soft. Leave to cool slightly then cut the eggplants in half lengthways and scoop out the flesh.

4) Heat the oil in a large, heavy frying pan, add the eggplants flesh and fry for 5 minutes. Put the eggplants mixture into a food processor, add the lemon juice and blend until smooth. Gradually add the yogurt, then the garlic and cumin. Season with salt and pepper.

5) Pour the mixture into a serving bowl and chill in the refrigerator for at least 1 hour.

6) Garnish with chopped fresh parsley and pomegranate seeds! Serve with strips of raw pepper or sesame crackers.

7. Warak Al Mashwi - Stuffed Vine leaves

These stuffed grape leaves are a delicious, light, and healthy treat, with a tasty combination of vegetables and rice steamed in a savory lemon and olive oil broth. They are excellent for outdoor parties, the beach, or as a poolside snack!

Total Time: 2h + 5h resting time.

Serves: 30 rolls

Ingredients:

Filling -

- 1 pound coarsely ground lamb (from the leg)
- 1 cup converted (also called parboiled) rice
- 1½ tsp salt
- ½ tsp black pepper
- 1 tsp ground allspice
- ½ tsp ground cinnamon
- ½ cup melted butter
- ½ cup and ½ cup cold water, divided
- 1 (16-ounce) jar grape leaves

Seasoning –

- 1 tsp salt
- ¼ tsp black pepper
- ½ tsp allspice
- ¼ tsp ground cinnamon
- 1 tbsp. extra-virgin olive oil
- ¼ cup freshly squeezed lemon juice
- 2¾ cups boiling water

Instructions:

1. Combine all the filling ingredients plus ½ cup water in a bowl. Mix well, cover and refrigerate. After 30 minutes, remove from the refrigerator and add the second ½ cup of cold water.

2. To roll a grape leaf, take a leaf and place it flat on your work surface with the dull side (the side with raised veins) facing up and the stem end nearest to you. Place 1 level tbsp. of filling right above the stem base and distribute it lengthwise (about 2½ inches). Fold the bottom of the leaf up and over the filling, then fold the both sides (the right and left) of the leaf over the filling.

3. Tuck and roll the leaf tightly and evenly up toward the tip of the leaf and set the rolled grape leaf aside (with the seam facing down so it will not unravel). Repeat with the rest of the filling.

4. The rolled grape leaves should be about 2½ inches long. Reserve the extra pieces of grape leaves for later use.

5. Preheat the oven to 400°F. Lower one rack to the lowest shelf of the oven. Brush olive oil over the bottom of two 9-inch round cake pans. Arrange some of the reserved leaves to cover the bottom of the pans to prevent sticking while the grape leaves cook.

6. Load the stuffed grape leaves, starting from the side of the pan. Place one grape leaf in at a time, seam side down, end-to-end around the pan in concentric circles. Work your way toward the center, nestling one right next to the other. (Placing them close together will prevent them from unraveling while they steam.)

7. Prepare the seasoning by mixing all the ingredients together. Stir well and pour half over each pan of grape leaves. Cover and seal the top of each pan with aluminum foil.

8. Place the pans on a foil-lined baking sheet and bake on the lower rack of the oven for 1½ hours. Then set the grape leaves aside to cool for about 5 hours.

8. Tabbouleh – Tossed Bulgur Salad

Bulgur is one of the most popular foods in Lebanon. This refreshing, flavorful salad is very typical of Lebanese cuisine.

Total Time: 2h

Serves: 4

Ingredients:

- 2½ cups parsley, finely chopped
- 1 cup diced tomato (¼ inch)
- 1/3 cup green onion, finely chopped
- 2 tbsp. mint leaves, finely chopped
- ¼ cup bulgur wheat
- 3 tbsp. freshly squeezed lemon juice
- 4 tbsp. extra-virgin olive oil
- ½ tsp salt
- Pinch of sugar
- Pinch of paprika

- Pinch of black pepper

Instructions:

1. To prepare the salad, combine the first 5 ingredients in a bowl and mix well. Cover and refrigerate for at least 2 hours prior to serving (allowing the bulgur to expand). Add the next 6 ingredients and mix thoroughly just before serving.

9. Sambusak bi Jibn – Cheese Crescents

This pastry is simple to prepare and easy to handle. The crispy outer layers combined with the warm cheese filling are a perfect combination and make for a great party appetizer!

Total Time: 1h 30m

Serves: 24 Sambusak

Ingredients:

Dough -

- 1½ cups unbleached flour
- 6 tbsp. chilled butter, diced
- ¼ tsp salt
- ¼ cup and 1 tbsp. cold water
- 2 cups canola oil (for frying)

Filling –

- ¼ pound Bulgarian feta cheese, crumbled
- ¼ cup minced yellow onion
- ¼ cup finely chopped parsley;
- ¼ tsp salt
- ¼ tsp coarsely ground black pepper

Instructions:

1. To prepare the sambusak pastry, combine the flour, butter, and salt in a bowl. Using a pastry blender in a rocking motion, cut the butter into the flour by pressing it up against the sides and the bottom of the bowl until all the pieces of butter have been cut in and the mixture resembles cornmeal. (If you do not have a pastry blender, use the tines of a fork to press the butter into the flour; it takes a bit longer, but it will work.)

2. Add the cold water, mixing quickly with your hand to form the dough. Shape the dough into a disc about 1 inch thick. Wrap the disc in plastic wrap and refrigerate; this allows the dough to rest. After 1 hour, remove the dough from the refrigerator and let it stand for 10 minutes at room temperature prior to rolling.

3. To prepare the filling, separately press the feta cheese and onion between paper towels until they are dry. Combine the feta cheese, onion, parsley, salt, and pepper in a bowl. Use the tines of a fork to mix the ingredients until they are well combined. Portion the cheese into 1 tsp, egg-shaped balls and place them on a plate double-lined with paper towels to absorb excess liquid. Loosely cover with plastic wrap and refrigerate until needed. Remove the filling from the refrigerator 10 minutes prior to preparing the crescents.

4. To prepare the crescents, on a lightly floured surface, roll the dough out to 1⁄8-inch thickness. Cut the dough into 2½-inch rounds using a cookie cutter; make one cut directly next to the other to maximize the number of rounds.

5. Cover the rounds with plastic wrap to avoid drying. Pick up 1 round at a time and flip it over so that you are placing the filling on the underside of the dough (or whichever side seems stickier). Place a portion of cheese in the center. Fold the dough over the cheese so it forms a half-moon crescent. Firmly pinch the edges together with your fingers, securing the cheese inside while forming an outer rim ¼ inch wide. (Avoid getting cheese trapped in between the edges; this may cause the crescents to open later.)

6. Fill the remaining rounds.

7. Place the crescents flat on your work surface. Using the tines of a fork, press firmly along the outer rim of each crescent to crimp the edges, locking the cheese inside. Be careful not to pierce the dough. Alternatively, you can crimp the edges as you would a piecrust.

8. Heat the oil to 375°F in a small saucepan over medium-high heat, using a candy/fry thermometer for accuracy. The oil should be about 1 inch deep. Fry 6 crescents at a time until golden brown, then transfer to a plate double-lined with paper towels. Fry the remaining crescents. Make sure the temper

9. Make sure the oil remains at 375°F so that the crescents fry evenly. Let them cool for several minutes prior to serving.

Mains

10. Mujaddara – Lentils with Rice and Caramelized Onions

Mujaddara is a delicious staple meal in Lebanese cuisine. The caramelized onions enhance the rich texture and color of the pureed lentils making it a hearty and filling meal!

Total Time: 1h

Serves: 4-6

Ingredients:

- 8 ounces brown lentils (about 1¼ cups)
- 1 tsp and ¾ tsp salt, divided
- ¼ cup basmati rice
- 1/3 cup and 1 tbsp. extra-virgin olive oil, divided
- 3 cups diced yellow onion (¼ inch)

Instructions:

1. Check the lentils and discard any stones or debris. Place them in a fine-

mesh sieve and rinse under cold running water for about 30 seconds.

2. Place the lentils, 4½ cups water, and 1 tsp salt in a medium pot over high heat, uncovered. Bring to a rolling boil, then reduce heat to medium and simmer covered for 25 minutes. Test a couple of lentils to make sure they are tender. If they seem crunchy, continue to cook them until tender.

3. Place the rice and ¾ cup water in a small saucepan over high heat, uncovered. Once it comes to a boil, reduce heat to medium-low and simmer covered for 10 minutes or until the water is absorbed. Remove from the heat and set aside, covered.

4. Drain the beans through a fine-mesh sieve and reserve ½ cup of the liquid. Set the pot aside for later use.

5. Place the cooked lentils and the reserved liquid in a food processor fitted with a metal blade. Pulse several times (do not over process) until the lentils are evenly ground. Return them to the pot and set aside.

6. Double-line a dish with paper towels and set it aside. Preheat 1/3 cup olive oil in a medium skillet over medium-high heat. Add the onions and ¾ tsp salt, and sauté until the onions are evenly reddish brown and caramelized. Remove the skillet from the heat, tilt it to one side, and use a slotted spoon to slide half of the onions to the top of the pan. Use the back of the spoon to press out as much oil as you can from the onions (pressing the oil out makes them crispier). Transfer the caramelized onions to the paper towel–lined dish and spread them out evenly; set aside.

7. Set the skillet over medium-high heat and gradually add ½ cup water (caution: it will splatter) followed by the cooked basmati rice. Cook, uncovered, stirring occasionally, until the water is absorbed. Stir this mixture into the pureed lentils.

8. Place the mixture of lentils and onions over medium low heat and cook uncovered for 3 to 5 minutes, then stir in 1 tbsp. olive oil. Remove from the heat.

9. Spread the pureed lentils evenly over a shallow platter. Set aside to cool for several hours loosely covered with waxed paper. Once cooled, sprinkle most of the caramelized onions around the perimeter, and a few in the center, and serve!

11. Tamiya - Falafel Sandwich

A staple snack in Middle East countries, Falafels are best enjoyed on a cold rainy evening. The spices combined with the crunch make for a delicious snack. Add them to a pita bread and you get a very filling meal perfect for quick lunch on the go!

Total Time: 30m

Serves: 5

Ingredients:

Falafels –

- ½ lb. green lentils
- 3 tbsp. fresh cilantro, finely chopped
- 3 green chilies, chopped
- 2 onions, chopped
- 2 cloves garlic, crushed
- ½ tsp baking powder
- 1 tsp zatar (substitute with thyme or oregano)

- Oil for frying
- Salt to taste

Sandwich –

- 5 pieces pita Bread
- ¾ cup tahini Sauce
- 2 hardboiled eggs, sliced
- 1 eggplant, sliced and deep fried.
- ½ cup white cabbage, finely chopped
- ½ cup diced pickled turnips

Instructions:

1. Soak the dal in water overnight. Combine with the chilies, garlic and cilantro leaves in a food processor and process into a thick paste. Add salt.

2. Add in the onions, zatar, and baking powder and mix well.

3. Take about 2 spoons of mixture and roll it into a ball. Flatten slightly. Do this with the rest of the batter.

4. Heat oil in a pan. Deep fry the falafels until golden brown. Remove and allow to cool slightly.

5. To assemble the sandwich, cut the pita bread pieces into half.

6. Heat the pita bread slightly and top with falafels, tahini sauce, egg slices, eggplant slices, cabbage, and radishes.

7. Serve immediately with extra tahini sauce!

12. Chicken Shawarma

Shawarma has been a staple street food throughout the Middle East. Juicy grilled chicken atop soft pita bread with a delicious garlic sauce all rolled with fresh greens makes for a quick and easy dinner!

Total Time: 40m + resting time

Serves: 8

Ingredients:

Chicken -

- 2.5 lb. skinless boneless chicken breasts
- 1/3 cup lemon juice
- 2 tbsp. tomato paste
- 4 tbsp. Greek yogurt
- 2 tbsp. white vinegar
- 1 head garlic, crushed
- 2 tbsp. olive oil
- 1 to 1.5 tsp salt (to taste)
- ½ tsp ground oregano (or thyme)
- 1 tsp paprika

- ½ tsp ginger powder (optional)
- A pinch of nutmeg powder

Garlic Sauce –

- 2 heads of garlic, peeled
- 2-2 ½ cup vegetable oil
- ½ lemon, freshly juiced
- ½ teaspoon of salt (or to taste)

Shawarma -

- 8 pita bread pieces
- 2 tomatoes, chopped and grilled
- 4 pickled cucumbers, cut lengthwise
- French Fries (optional)
- ½ cup shredded lettuce

Instructions:

1. To make the garlic sauce, ensure all ingredients are at room temperature.

2. In a food processor, add the garlic and salt. Process till the garlic turns almost pasty looking. Make sure you scrape the sides of the processor a few times while processing.

3. Once the garlic looks completely crushed, we can start adding in the oil. Leave the processor on until the end. Start slowly adding the oil in a very thin stream, ½ cup at a time. After the first batch of oil, very carefully add in ½ tsp of lemon juice. Allow the paste to absorb the lemon juice before adding in the next ½ cup of oil. Repeat the steps with the rest of the oil and lemon juice, being sure to be careful and slow the entire team.

4. Move to a bowl and set aside for later use.

5. Rinse the chicken breasts with fresh cold water then cut lengthwise into thin cuts of about ½ inch.

6. In a large bowl, combine the rest of the ingredients together and add in the chicken. Cover and marinate in the fridge overnight.

7. To prepare, preheat a Panini grill or a portable grill. You can also cook the chicken on a grill pan on the stove.

8. Grill for about 15 minutes on medium heat. Once cooked shred the chicken

in thin pieces.

9. To make the shawarma, spread some garlic sauce onto a pita bread. Add in some of the chicken and top with pickles, fries, lettuce and tomatoes.

10. Roll tightly and enjoy!

13. Kousa Mashi – Stuffed Zucchinis

This delicious dish is made of tender zucchinis stuffed with a spiced meat mixture and cooked off in a hearty tomato sauce! This is best served with a side of Basmati rice!

Total Time: 1h

Serves: 6

Ingredients:

- 2 lb. Zucchini
- 5 tsp oil
- 2 large onions, finely chopped
- 1 chili
- ½ cup fresh parsley, chopped
- 1 lb. minced meat

- 1 tbsp. meat spice
- 1 tsp soft cinnamon
- 1 tsp dried thyme
- 1 tsp dried mint
- 1 tsp dried basil
- 2 tbsp. tomato paste
- 2 cups water
- 1 tbsp. salt
- 1 tbsp. black pepper
- 2 large tomatoes, diced

Instructions:

1. Cut the zucchinis in half, and scoop out the pulp and seeds, leaving about ¼ inch of the rind intact.

2. In a large pan, heat a little oil and fry the zucchinis until for a few minutes until brown. Then remove from the pan and set aside.

3. In the same pan, add in the onions and chili. Season with salt to taste. Cook until the unions turn a soft golden brown.

4. Add in the minced meat and cook for 3 minutes, stirring constantly. Add in the parsley leaves and spices. Cover the pan and let cook for about 20 minutes.

5. Stuff the zucchinis with the meat mixture and place in a baking tray.

6. In a small pan, combine the tomato paste with 2 cups of water and season with salt and pepper. Bring to a boil.

7. Add in the diced tomatoes and continue boiling for 2 minutes. Remove from heat.

8. Pour in 1tbsp. of the tomato mixture onto each zucchini and then pour the rest into the baking pan. Cover with a lid or aluminum foil.

9. Place the baking pan onto the stove and cook for 20 minutes on high. As it cooks, preheat oven to 400 F.

10. After 20 minutes, place the pan into the oven for 15 minutes to cook through. Make sure the zucchini is tender and soft.

11. Transfer to a serving platter or individual plates and serve!

14. Beef Shawarma

This beef shawarma differs in flavor to the chicken shawarma with the use of the tangy tahini sauce! Spiced meet, tangy sauce and fresh veggies rolled together in soft bread? Sign us up!

Total Time: 40m + resting time

Serves: 8

Ingredients:

Marinade -

- 3 lb. fatty beef cuts
- 10 cloves garlic
- ¾ cup freshly squeezed lemon juice
- 1/3 cup apple cider vinegar
- 1/3 cup olive oil
- 2 tsp cloves
- 2 tsp salt

- 1 tsp cumin
- 1 tsp caraway
- 1 tsp cardamom
- 1 tsp of oregano or thyme
- 1 tsp cinnamon
- 1 tsp nutmeg
- 1 tsp crushed peppercorn
- 1 tsp of cayenne pepper
- 1 tsp ground ginger

Tahini Sauce –

- 4 teaspoons tahini paste
- 1 cup freshly squeezed Lemon Juice
- 6 gloves garlic, crushed
- Dash of salt
- Sandwich Ingredients
- 1 cup fresh parsley, finely chopped
- 3 Grilled tomatoes
- French fries
- 8 Pita bread pieces
- 4 pickled cucumbers, cut lengthwise

Instructions:

1. Cut the beef into strips about 4 inches long and at a thickness of ½ inch.

2. Combine the marinade ingredients together in a bowl and add in the beef. Allow to marinate overnight in the refrigerator.

3. To make the tahini sauce, combine all the sauce ingredients together in a bowl and whisk well to mix.

4. To cook the beef, heat up a Panini grill or a grill pan on medium high heat. Grill the beef for 10-15 minutes or until cooked through. Allow to cool for 2 minutes before shredding the meet.

5. To make the shawarma, place some of the cooked beef onto a pita bread and drizzle with the tahini sauce. Top with grill tomatoes, pickles, parsley and French fries.

6. Roll tightly and serve warm!

15. Samkeh Harra – Spiced Baked Fish

Moist whole fish is covered with a spiced onion mixture giving you a delicious and cook dinner option that the whole family will love!

Total Time: 30m

Serves: 4

Ingredients:

- 2 lb. whole fish, scaled and cleaned
- 2 onions, sliced
- 4 cloves garlic, crushed
- 1 cup fresh parsley, chopped
- 1 cup fresh cilantro, chopped
- 1 tbsp. coriander powder
- ¼ - ½ tsp chili powder
- 3 tbsp. lemon juice
- 3 tbsp. oil
- Salt and pepper
- Chopped parsley and lemon wedges for garnish

Instructions:

1. Preheat oven to 450 F.

2. Heat oil in a pan. Add the fish and fry for 2 minutes on each side to crisp up the skin. Remove and place in a baking pan.

3. Add the onions to the same pan and cook till soft.

4. Add in the rest of the ingredients and cook for a few more minutes.

5. Spread this onion mixture onto the fish and inside it.

6. Add 1 cup of water to the baking pan and bake in the oven for 20 minutes or until fish has cooked through.

7. Serve sprinkled with fresh parsley and lemon wedges!

16. Shish Tawook – Grilled Chicken on Skewers

This simple marinade infuses chicken with great flavor. Infused with a delicious combination of yogurt, lemon and spices, the chunks of grilled chicken are super moist and tender.

Total Time: 30m + resting time

Serves: 6

Ingredients:

- ¼ cup plain yogurt
- 1 tbsp. lemon zest
- ¼ cup freshly squeezed lemon juice
- ¼ cup minced yellow onion
- 1 packed tbsp. peeled and grated fresh ginger (use the large holes of a grater)
- ¼ cup ketchup
- 1 tsp salt
- ¼ tsp coarsely ground black pepper
- ½ tsp ground allspice
- ¼ tsp ground cinnamon

- 1¼ pounds trimmed boneless skinless chicken breast, cut into 1½ x 1½-inch pieces (about 20 pieces)
- 1 tbsp. apple cider vinegar

Instructions:

1. Combine the first 10 ingredients in a bowl; mix well and set aside. Rinse the chicken in 1 cup cold water with the vinegar to refresh the flavor of the chicken, then drain.

2. Cut the chicken into 1½ x 1½-inch pieces. Add the chicken to the marinade and mix well. Cover and refrigerate for at least 6 hours or overnight prior to loading them on the skewers.

3. Load each skewer by piercing pieces of chicken onto the skewer. Pour any remaining marinade over the skewers.

4. Preheat the grill on medium-high heat. Grill for about 3 to 3½ minutes on one side. Flip the skewers and grill an additional 3 to 3½ minutes. Make sure the meat is cooked through but still moist before removing from the heat. Wrap the skewers in foil and allow them to steam for 4 to 6 minutes prior to serving.

5. Garnish with fresh parsley and serve!

17. Shush Barak – Meat Tortellini in Yogurt Sauce

Homemade tortellini cooked in a garlic-cilantro-laced yogurt sauce are easy to prepare and absolutely delicious. Offer this dish as a starter before a meal or as part of a buffet. Your friends and family will be intrigued by the delightful combination of flavors

Total Time: 1h 30m

Serves: 4

Ingredients:

Dough –

- 1¼ cups unbleached flour
- ¼ tsp salt
- 6 tbsp. water

Filling –

- 3 tbsp. pine nuts
- 1 tsp melted butter
- 1 tbsp. extra virgin olive oil
- ¼ pound ground beef

- 1 cup yellow onion, finely diced
- 1 tbsp. freshly squeezed lemon juice
- ½ tsp salt
- ¼ tsp coarsely ground black pepper
- ½ tsp allspice
- ¼ tsp cinnamon

Yogurt Sauce –

- 4 cups plain yogurt
- 2½ tbsp. cornstarch dissolved in 2 tbsp. cold water
- ½ tsp tahini (optional)
- 3 large cloves garlic mashed with 1 tsp salt
- 1 tbsp. butter
- 1 tsp ground coriander
- 1/3 cup finely chopped cilantro; use green leafy parts and tender stems
- 2 tbsp. freshly squeezed lemon juice

Instructions:

1. In a bowl, combine the flour, salt, and water. Mix and knead the dough, forming it into a ball shape. Wrap in plastic and set aside at room temperature for half an hour.

2. Preheat the oven to 350°F. Line a baking tray with aluminum foil and sprinkle on the pine nuts. Toast for 5-7 minutes in the center of the oven, occasionally tossing the nuts. Mix the melted butter with the nuts, then transfer to a paper towel– lined dish and set aside.

3. Preheat the olive oil in a small skillet over medium high heat. Add the ground meat and cook, breaking it into small minced pieces. Once the meat is no longer pink, add the onion, lemon juice, salt, and spices. Reduce heat to medium-low and cook uncovered until onions turn soft. Remove from the heat. Cool the filling completely before using.

4. Preheat the oven to 400°F. On a lightly floured surface, roll the dough out to 1/16-inch thickness. Cut the dough into 2½-inch rounds using a cookie cutter; cut the rounds one right next to the other to maximize the number of rounds. Cover them with plastic wrap to avoid drying. Lightly flour a foil lined baking sheet and place it within reach.

5. To fill the tortellini, pick up one round of dough at a time and flip it so that you are placing the filling on the underside (or whichever side seems stickier). Cradling the round of dough in one hand place ½ tbsp. cooled filling and 3 pine nuts in the center of the dough. Fold one side over to form a crescent shape and press well along the edges to secure the filling inside. Then wrap the crescent around your index finger and press the outer tips together, forming a ring shape.

6. Stand the ring-shaped tortellini on the tray, seam side down. Repeat with the remaining rounds of dough, placing the tortellini's ½ inch apart on the baking sheet.

7. Bake the tortellini on the middle rack in the oven, lightly shaking the tray occasionally, for 12 to 14 minutes, or until the edges brown. Remove and set aside.

8. Rinse a medium-sized pot with cold water (this will help prevent the yogurt from sticking while it cooks). Pass the yogurt through a fine-mesh strainer into the rinsed pot. Add the dissolved cornstarch and the tahini. Mix well and set aside.

9. Mash the garlic to a pulp with the salt using a mortar and pestle. Melt the butter in a small skillet over medium heat. Add the garlic pulp and sauté until it begins to sizzle (not brown). Remove from the heat. Stir in the coriander. Add this mixture to the yogurt.

10. Place the yogurt mixture over high heat, uncovered, and cook, using a flat-edged heat-proof spatula to continually stir and scrape the bottom and sides of the pot to ensure the yogurt does not stick. Once it boils, check to make sure there aren't any lumps; use a whisk to evenly dissolve any lumps until the mixture is smooth.

11. Add the baked tortellini, then the cilantro and lemon juice, and return the mixture to a boil, gently stirring with the flat-edged spatula to separate the tortellini from one another as they cook. Continue scraping the sides and the bottom of the pot. After 5 minutes, remove from the heat and set aside for 10 minutes, uncovered, prior to serving.

12. Garnish with fresh chopped cilantro and enjoy!

18. Moghrabieh – Lebanese Couscous

Lebanese couscous consists of larger dried beads made from flour, salt, and water, like pasta. These flavorful beads are steamed in a rich broth, then mixed with pearl onions and garbanzo beans.

Total Time: 3h

Serves: 6

Ingredients:

Chicken –

- 3 pounds split chicken breast (each breast cut into 3 pieces lengthwise)
- 2 tbsp. apple cider vinegar
- 4 tsp salt
- 1 cup diced yellow onion (1 inch)
- 1 rib celery (cut into 2-inch lengths)
- 1 (3- to 4-inch) stick cinnamon
- 1/2 tsp whole black peppercorns

- 1 tsp allspice
- 1 bay leaf
- 1/8 tsp ground cinnamon
- 1/8 tsp each of ground caraway

Bean – Onion Sauce –

- 2 cups diced yellow onion (1 inch)
- 1½ cups water
- ¼ tsp salt
- ½ tsp ground caraway
- ¼ tsp ground cinnamon
- 1 cup frozen pearl onions
- 1 (15- or 16-ounce) can garbanzo beans, drained 2 cups reserved broth

Couscous –

- 2 tbsp. extra-virgin olive oil
- 1½ cups Lebanese couscous (Can be found in your local Arab food store)
- ¼ tsp salt
- 1½ tsp ground caraway
- ½ tsp ground cinnamon
- 1 tbsp. butter

Instructions:

1. In a large pot, combine the chicken, and salt. Add in 12 cups of water and bring to a boil.

2. Skim any foam from the top and add in the remaining chicken ingredients. Reduce heat and allow to simmer for 45 minutes, stirring occasionally.

3. Using a slotted spoon, remove the chicken pieces and pass the broth through a fine-mesh sieve and return it to the pot. Add the chicken pieces back in and set aside.

4. In a medium-sized saucepan add diced onions, water, salt, ½ tsp caraway, and ¼ tsp cinnamon and bring to a boil.

5. Once it starts to boil, lower heat and allow to cook covered for 30 minutes. Then remove the cover and increase the heat to high, stirring frequently, until

most of the liquid evaporates. Remove from heat.

6. Use a whisk to mash the onions to a pulp. Add the pearl onions, garbanzo beans, and 2 cups of the chicken broth to the saucepan. Cook over high heat and bring to a boil. Lower heat, cover, and simmer for an additional 5 minutes, then remove from heat and set aside.

7. To prepare the couscous, preheat the olive oil in a large pot over medium high heat. Add the Lebanese couscous and cook, stirring constantly, evenly browning the couscous beads. Once the couscous beads begin to turn reddish brown, add the salt, caraway, and cinnamon. Mix well. Add 3 cups of the chicken broth and the butter.

8. Increase the heat to high and bring to a boil, then reduce heat to medium-low, cover, and simmer. After 15 minutes try a few beads to see if they are tender and the broth has been absorbed. If they are not tender and all the broth has been absorbed, add additional broth (1/4 cup at a time) and continue to cook until tender. Remove from the heat.

9. Use a slotted spoon to transfer the cooked garbanzo bean and pearl onion mixture from the sauce over the cooked couscous. Gently fold it into the couscous. Cover and set aside for 30 minutes, allowing the flavors to mingle and the couscous to expand.

10. Serve warm and enjoy!

19. Djaj ma Riz Boukhari – Cardamom Chicken with Rice

This delicious rice dish is packed full of flavor and is a guaranteed crowd pleaser! The meat is succulent and the rise is soft and fluffy, making this recipe a local favorite!

Total Time: 1h 30m

Serves: 4

Ingredients:

For chicken –

- 1 whole chicken, about 4½ pounds, cut into 10 pieces
- 2 tablespoons apple cider vinegar
- ¼ cup extra-virgin olive oil
- 1½ cups diced yellow onion (¼ inch)
- ½ cup peeled and shredded carrot (use the large holes of a grater)

- 2¾ teaspoons salt
- ¼ teaspoon coarsely ground black pepper
- ¾ teaspoons ground allspice
- ½ teaspoon ground cinnamon
- 2 teaspoons ground cumin
- 1 teaspoon ground cardamom
- 1/8 teaspoon ground cloves
- 1/16 teaspoon ground nutmeg
- 5 cups boiling water
- 1/3 cup tomato paste
- ¾ cup peeled and diced tomato (½ inch)

For Rice –

- 1 teaspoon extra-virgin olive oil
- 1 cup converted (also called parboiled) rice
- 2½ cups hot reserved broth
- ½ cup toasted slivered almonds
- ½ cup toasted golden raisins

Instructions:

1. Preheat the olive oil in a large pot. Add the onions, carrots, salt, and spices, and sauté over medium high heat for a couple of minutes. Add the pieces of chicken and cook until the meat is no longer pink.

2. Add the boiling water, tomato paste, and tomatoes. Stir well dissolving the tomato paste in the water. Increase the heat to high and bring the mixture to a rolling boil, uncovered, then reduce the heat to medium and simmer covered, stirring occasionally, for 25 minutes. Remove from the heat. Transfer the pieces of chicken to a flat tray and set aside to cool, uncovered. Reserve all of the broth.

3. To prepare the rice, heat the olive oil in a medium pot over medium heat. Stir in the rice and coat the grains. Add 2½ cups of the hot chicken broth and bring to a boil.

4. Once boiling, reduce heat and cook covered for 15 minutes or until the liquid has been absorbed.

5. Remove from heat and keep covered for 20 minutes.

6. To serve, arrange the rice on a platter with the pieces of meat around the

perimeter of the rice. Scatter the toasted nuts and raisins in the center and serve!

20. Dawood Basha – Meatballs in Tomato Sauce

If you like meatballs, you might want to try out these Lebanese meat kebabs in a flavorsome tomato sauce. Soft meatballs are covered in a spiced tomato sauce to make for a hearty, filling meal!

Total Time: 1h 30m

Serves: 4

Ingredients:

- 1 lb. lean, finely minced lamb
- 2 oz. fresh breadcrumbs
- 1 onion, finely chopped
- 1 garlic clove, crushed
- 3 tbsp. finely chopped fresh parsley
- 1 tsp ground cumin
- Salt and pepper
- 1 egg, beaten
- 2 tbsp. olive oil

Tomato Sauce –

- 1 28 oz. can chopped tomatoes in juice.
- ¼ tsp sugar
- 3 tbsp. olive oil
- 1 garlic clove, crushed
- ¼ tsp ground cumin
- 1 tbsp. chopped fresh parsley
- 1 bay leaf
- Salt and pepper
- ¼ cup pine nuts

Instructions:

1. To make the meatballs, put the minced lamb, breadcrumbs, onion, garlic, parsley, cumin, cinnamon, salt and pepper in a bowl and mix together.

2. Stir in the beaten egg, then knead the mixture for about 5 minutes or until it forms a paste. Chill in the refrigerator for about 1 hour.

3. Meanwhile, prepare the tomato sauce. Put all the ingredients in a large saucepan (it needs to be large enough to hold the sausages in a single layer). Bring to the boil, then simmer for about 30 minutes.

4. With dampened hands, form the lamb mixture into 12 equal-sized meatballs. Heat the oil in a large frying pan, add the sausages and fry for 15 minutes or until browned on all sides.

5. Using a slotted spoon, transfer the sausages to the pan containing the tomato sauce and simmer for 10-15 minutes. Garnish with pine nuts.

6. Serve warm with Basmati rice and enjoy!

21. Djaj bil Furrin – Roasted Lemon-Garlic Chicken

This recipe is easy to prepare and delivers a lot of flavor. A combination of fresh lemon juice, garlic, onions, and olive oil set the stage for this dish that will leave you wanting more!

Total Time: 1h + resting time

Serves: 8

Ingredients:

- 1 whole chicken, cut into 10 pieces
- 2 tablespoons apple cider vinegar
- 5 large cloves garlic
- 1½ teaspoons salt
- ¼ cup cloves garlic (cut in half lengthwise)

- 1 tablespoon lemon zest
- ½ cup freshly squeezed lemon juice
- 2 lemons (cut each into 6 wedges)
- 2 tablespoons extra-virgin olive oil
- ½ cup grated yellow onion
- ¼ teaspoon table-grind black pepper
- Lemon wedges, sprigs of parsley, and paprika (for garnish)

Instructions:

1. Place the 5 large cloves of garlic in the same large bowl with the salt and use a pestle to mash it to a pulp. Add the remaining ingredients (not the garnish) and mix well. Add the chicken and fully coat the pieces. Cover and refrigerate overnight.

2. Preheat the oven to 450°F. Place the pieces of chicken, skin-side up, in an ovenproof baking dish just large enough to hold them. Place the legs and thighs toward the outer edge of the dish and the breasts and wings toward the center. Wedge the pieces of lemon and garlic between the pieces of chicken. Pour the remaining marinade over the top. Bake on the middle rack of the oven for 40 to 45 minutes, basting the chicken a couple of times.

3. To brown the chicken, place under the broiler until golden brown. Keep a watchful eye, as it will brown quickly under the broiler. Remove from the oven and let stand for 10 minutes prior to serving.

4. Serve warm with a side of Batata bil Furren!

Sides

22. Ka'ak Bread – Lebanese Bagel

The Lebanese version of a bagel, this bread has a crispy exterior with a soft fluffy inside making it perfect for snack time or to have with your tea! Try it with a spread of Greek yogurt!

Total Time: 2h + resting time

Serves: 2 loaves

Ingredients:

- ½ cup whole wheat flour
- ¾ tbsp. sugar
- 1 ¾ all-purpose flour
- 1 tsp. salt
- 1 tbsp. instant yeast
- ½ cup buttermilk
- ½ cup water

- 1 tbsp. olive oil
- 1 small egg
- ½ tbsp. water
- 1/8 tsp sugar
- Pinch of salt
- 1 tbsp. sesame seeds
- 1 tbsp. black seeds.

Instructions:

1. Combine the first 5 dry ingredients. In the bowl of a stand mixer. Add in the buttermilk, water, and oil. Mix together with a dough hook for 9 minutes. Transfer to a greased bowl, cover with damp towel and allow to rest for an hour.

2. Meanwhile, line a baking tray with baking paper. In a large pan, add in about an inch of water and set in the bottom row of your oven.

3. Lightly flour your work space. Remove dough and divide into 2 equal pieces.

4. Start by rolling out a piece of dough into a log about 8 inches in length. Start rolling out the ends of the log so that they are thinner and longer than the rest of the dough. Fold both sides upwards and pinch to join together. You should have something resembling a "purse".

5. Using your hands, lightly press down on the thicker part of the log to flatten it out to ¾ inches thickness. Cover loosely with plastic wrap. Repeat with other piece. Lay onto the prepared baking tray.

6. Let rise for another 45 minutes. At 15 minutes left to go, whisk together the egg, water, salt, and sugar in a bowl. Set aside. Preheat oven to 425 F.

7. Once the dough has risen ready, coat with the egg wash and sprinkle on the seeds.

8. Bake the loaves, for 15 to 18 minutes, until golden brown.

9. Cool the loaves on a wire rack for at least 10 minutes. Enjoy while still warm!

23. Shorbat Adas – Lentil Soup

This full-bodied soup is a traditional dish for iftar, the evening meal during Ramadan. Many ingredients—such as rice, ground lamb or beef, chickpeas, or beans—can be added to this simple soup.

Total Time: 1h

Serves: 4

Ingredients:

- 1 c. red lentils, split
- 6 c. water
- 2 cubes chicken bouillon
- 2 tbsp. olive oil
- 1 medium onion, chopped
- salt and pepper to taste

Instructions:

1. Wash and drain lentils. In a large pot, combine the lentils and water and bring to a boil.

2. Reduce heat, cover, and simmer.

3. While lentils are simmering, heat olive oil in a skillet over high heat. Sauté onion in oil until golden brown.

4. Add onions, salt, and pepper to lentils.

5. Continue simmering for 25 to 35 minutes, or until lentils are soft. Serve hot with lemon wedges and pita bread.

24. Ruz Basmati Adas - Basmati Rice with Cumin, Lentils, and Onion

The fragrance that fills the air while preparing this rice is heavenly. This long-grained rice is well known for the perfume-like aroma it releases as it steams.

Total Time: 1h 20m

Serves: 4

Ingredients:

Rice -

- 1 cup basmati rice
- 2 cups water
- ½ tsp salt
- 1 tbsp. butter

Other -

- ¼ cup lentils
- 3 cups water
- ¼ tsp and
- ½ tsp salt, divided
- 3 tbsp. extra-virgin olive oil
- ½ cup diced yellow onion (¼ inch)
- ¼ cup golden raisins
- ¼ cup coarsely chopped green onion; use light and dark green parts
- ¾ tsp cumin

Instructions:

1. Rinse the rice in a fine-mesh strainer under cold running water for about 15 seconds. Drain well.

2. Stir the rice, water, salt, and butter together in a medium saucepan and bring to a boil over high heat, uncovered. Once it comes to a rolling boil, reduce heat to medium-low and simmer covered for 10 minutes, or until all the moisture is absorbed. Remove from the heat and set aside, covered. After 20 minutes luff with a fork, separating the grains.

3. Prepare the plain Basmati Rice as described on page 132 and set it aside for 20 minutes prior to folding in the cumin-lentil-onion mixture.

4. Meanwhile, place the lentils, water, and ¼ tsp salt in a medium saucepan over high heat, uncovered. Bring to a rolling boil, then reduce heat to medium-high and cook uncovered for 10 to 12 minutes or until the lentils are tender. Drain the lentils and set them aside, uncovered.

5. Preheat the olive oil in the same medium saucepan over medium heat. Add the yellow onion and ½ tsp salt, and sauté until the onions are tender. Add the raisins and cook them until they seem inflated. Then add the green onions, cumin, and drained lentils. Mix together for about a minute. Pour this mixture over the prepared rice, and gently fold it into the rice using a flexible spatula. Serve lightly warm or at room temperature.

25. Makhlouta – Bean Soup

A delightful and delicious combination of flavors and textures are brought together in this soup. So simple to prepare, it is slow-cooked with browned onions and cumin for a unique and distinct flavor. The beans provide a good source of nutrients, including iron and protein.

Total Time: 1h 45m

Serves: 4

Ingredients:

- 1 cup dry bean soup mix (15- or 16-bean soup mix)
- ¾ tsp and ½ tsp salt, divided
- 2 tbsp. extra-virgin olive oil
- 2 tbsp. butter
- 2 cups diced yellow onion (¼ inch)

- 1/8 tsp coarsely ground black pepper
- 1½ tsp cumin
- 1/3 cup brown lentils
- 2½ cups boiling water

Instructions:

1. Rinse the bean soup mix in a bowl, changing the water 3 times, and drain. Place the soup mix, ¾ tsp salt, and 4 cups water over high heat and cover. Bring to a boil.

2. Once it starts boiling, spoon off any foam off the top. Reduce heat to medium-low and simmer covered for 30 to 40 minutes.

3. In the meantime, preheat the oil and butter in a skillet over medium-high heat. Add the onions, 1/2 tsp salt, and the pepper, and sauté the onions until they are tender and slightly browned, then add the cumin and mix well. Remove from the heat and set aside.

4. When the beans are slightly tender, add the lentils and continue to cook covered for about 20 minutes.

5. Add the boiling water to the browned onions and mix well. Pour this mixture over the beans and continue to cook, covered, for 10 to 15 minutes. Check to make certain the beans are tender, then remove the stew from the heat. Set aside to cool for 10 to 15 minutes prior to serving.

26. Batata bil Furren - Roasted Onion-Cumin Potato Wedges

Crisp spears of oven-roasted potatoes coated with olive oil, onion, paprika, and cumin are hard to resist. The crunchy texture of the seasonings on the outside of the potato is absolutely delicious.

Total Time: 30m

Serves: 6

Ingredients:

- 4 russet potatoes, about ½ pound each, rinsed well, cut lengthwise (8 spears each)
- 3 tablespoons extra-virgin olive oil

- 3 tablespoons granulated onion (not powdered)
- 1½ teaspoons ground paprika
- 2 teaspoons ground cumin
- 1 teaspoon salt

Instructions:

1. Preheat your oven to 450°F. Combine the potato spears in a large bowl with the rest of the ingredients. Mix well to coat the individual spears.

2. Arrange the spears side-by-side, skin-side down, on a foil-lined baking sheet. Roast in the top of the oven for 15 minutes, then move the sheet to the middle rack for an additional 8 to 10 minutes or until brown and crisp on the outside.

3. Remove from the oven, platter, and serve.

Desserts

27. Kanafa – Semolina Cream Pie

Two layers of crispy, shredded dough surround a warm cheesy center, topped off with a sweet syrup make up this delicious Lebanese dessert. It is the perfect ending to a great meal or even as an afternoon sweet with tea.

Total Time: 1h

Serves: 8

Ingredients:

Kanafa -

- 1 ½ cups semolina
- ¼ cup + 2 tbsp. clarified butter or ghee
- 1 cup Akkawi Cheese (Can be substituted with Mozzarella and Ricotta cheese at a ratio of 4:3)
- 1 tbsp. sugar
- 1 tbsp. milk

- 1 tsp. rose water
- 2 tbsp. water
- Chopped pistachios for decoration

Sugar Syrup –
- 1 cup sugar
- ½ cup water
- 1 tsp lemon juice
- ½ tsp vanilla extract

Instructions:

1. Soak Akkawi cheese (or if using substitute, soak only Mozzarella) in warm water for 30 minutes. Drain and allow to dry before grating.

2. Preheat oven to 350 F.

3. In a large pan, combine the semolina, ghee, sugar, milk, rose water, and water. Mix thoroughly.

4. Spread the semolina mixture into a large baking pan and bake in the oven for 10 minutes, until slightly browned. Remove and allow to cool.

5. Once cooled, start breaking up the mixture. You can do this by hand, crushing the dough into fine crumbs or roughly process large chunks in a food processor.

6. Butter an 8 inch baking pan and press in 2/3 of the semolina crumbs into the pan, forming a base. Make sure to go up to the edges as well.

7. Sprinkle in the cheese and cover with the remaining 1/3 of the semolina crumbs.

8. Bake at 350 F for 30 minutes or until the crust turns a golden brown.

9. As the Kanafa bakes, prepare the sugar syrup.

10. In a saucepan, combine the sugar, water, and lemon juice. Bring to a boil. Do not stir as this will cause sugar crystallization.

11. As soon as the mixture comes to a boil, lower the heat and cook for 10 minutes. Remove from heat and add in the vanilla. Allow to cool.

12. Once the Kanafa has cooked through, remove from oven and pour over 2/3rd of the syrup on immediately. Allow to cool for 10 minutes before flipping over onto a serving dish.

13. Serve with additional sugar syrup on the side!

28. Mouhallabiyeh – Milk Pudding

This unique and delicious dessert is a wonderful combination of rose and orange blossom waters, infused into a smooth and creamy pudding. You can add cardamom for a subtle change in flavor or substitute vanilla essence in place of the rose and orange blossom water. Apricots, almonds, and pistachios top this pudding, complementing the overall flavor.

Total Time: 1h

Serves: 6

Ingredients:

Garnish –

- 2 tbsp. toasted slivered almonds
- ½ tbsp. melted butter
- 6 dried apricots
- 1½ cups water
- ¼ cup sugar
- 1 tbsp. finely ground pistachios (unsalted)

Pudding –

- 4 cups milk

- 7 tbsp. rice flour dissolved in 1/3 cup plus 1 tbsp. cold water
- ½ cup sugar
- 1½ tsp orange blossom water
- 1½ tsp rose water

Instructions:

1. Preheat the oven to 350°F. Spread the almonds over a foil-lined baking sheet and toast in the center of the oven, occasionally shaking the pan, for 5 to 7 minutes or until golden brown. Mix the melted butter with the nuts. Transfer to a paper towel–lined dish and set aside to cool.

2. Place the apricots, 1½ cups water, and sugar in a small saucepan over high heat and bring to a rolling boil. Reduce heat to medium-low, cover, and simmer for 20 minutes. Remove from the heat and set aside to cool completely before using.

3. To prepare the pudding, rinse a medium pot with cold water (this will help prevent the milk from sticking). Add the milk to the pot, place it over high heat, and bring to a boil uncovered. Use a flat-edged, heat-proof spatula to constantly stir and scrape the bottom and sides of the pot to prevent the milk from sticking and burning.

4. Once the milk comes to a boil, remove it from the heat. Add the dissolved rice flour, constantly stirring the mixture to prevent lumps. Return the pot to medium heat uncovered, and continue cooking, stirring constantly, using a whisk to break down any lumps that may appear.

5. After 4 to 6 minutes the pudding will thicken. Once it coats the spatula, drop 1 tsp of pudding on a saucer and set it aside to cool for 1 minute (meanwhile stirring the pudding). Turn the saucer sideways; if the pudding remains in place, add the sugar to the pot, stirring to dissolve the sugar.

6. After 2 to 4 minutes, place another tsp of pudding on the saucer and repeat the test. If it stays, add in the orange or rose waters. Cook the pudding for 2 more minutes, then pour it into a shallow, heat-proof serving dish. Cool completely, uncovered. Place in the refrigerator for 30 minutes.

7. Once chilled, garnish with the apricots and nuts and serve!

29. Asaibi Zainab – Crispy Almond fingers

Layers of filo dough wrapped around ground almonds scented with orange blossom water, this crunchy treat will quickly become a favorite around your home. These sweet crispy fingers are easy to make and are absolutely delicious.

Total Time: 1h 20m

Serves: 40 fingers

Ingredients:

Filo Fingers -

- 16 large sheets filo dough (room temperature)
- ¾ cup syrup
- 2 cups finely ground almonds
- 3 tbsp. sugar

- 1 tbsp. orange blossom water
- 1 cup melted clarified butter or ghee
- 2 tbsp. finely ground unsalted pistachios

Sugar Syrup –
- 1 cup sugar
- ½ cup water
- 1 tsp lemon juice
- ½ tsp vanilla extract

Instructions:

1. In a saucepan, combine the sugar, water, and lemon juice. Bring to a boil. Do not stir as this will cause sugar crystallization. As soon as the mixture comes to a boil, lower the heat and cook for 10 minutes. Remove from heat and add in the vanilla. Allow to cool.

2. Combine the almonds and sugar in a bowl. Mix in the orange blossom water, using the back of a spoon to press the orange blossom water into the almonds and sugar until evenly blended and the nuts seem damp. Set aside.

3. Preheat the oven to 325°F. On a flat surface, butter and layer 2 sheets of filo, placing them lengthwise, one at a time, one on top of the other. (The long side of the filo should be facing you from left to right.) Brush each sheet with butter by starting at the corners and edges and working your way to the center.

4. Lift the bottom left and right corners up, folding the layered filo in half lengthwise, making the dimension of the filo 17 inches long and about 6 inches wide. The seam side should be towards you.

5. Place 3 tablespoons almond filling in a line lengthwise (along the 17 inch length) from left to right, ½ inch above the seam. Use your fingers to distribute the filling evenly. Then fold the seam over the walnuts, securing them inside. Tightly and evenly roll the filo toward the top.

6. Brush the entire outside of the 17-inch roll with butter (to prevent drying and cracking), then transfer it to a foil-lined baking sheet and place it seam-side down (this will prevent the roll from unraveling as it bakes). Repeat with the remaining filo, placing each roll right up against the other, seam-side down. Cut each 17-inch roll into 5 fingers, equal in length (40 fingers total).

7. Place the tray on the middle rack of the oven and bake 35 to 45 minutes, or

until the rolls are golden brown (check the bottoms to make sure they have browned). Remove from the oven and drizzle the cool syrup over them. Garnish the tops with ground pistachios. Cool completely. Serve at room temperature.

30. Sfouf – Turmeric Cakes

These small cakes are a tasty snack, delicious with a warm cup of tea or a glass of milk. The secret ingredient? Turmeric! This deep yellow spice may not be what you would expect to find in a sweet tea cake but it does lend a spice note that is quite delicious!

Total Time: 45m

Serves: 18 small pieces

Ingredients:

Cake –

- 1 tbsp. tahini, mixed well (butter will do)
- 1½ cups Wondra flour (Any instant flour will do)
- ½ cup unbleached flour
- ¼ cup powdered milk
- 1 tbsp. turmeric
- 1 cup and 2 tbsp. granulated sugar
- 1½ tsp double-acting baking powder

- ¾ cup extra-virgin olive oil
- 2/3 cup water
- 2 tbsp. pine nuts

Instructions:

1. Preheat oven to 350°F. Spread the tahini over the bottom and sides of a 9-inch round pan.

2. In a bowl, mix together dry ingredients. Make a well in the center, then add the olive oil and water. Mix the batter thoroughly, using a flexible spatula.

3. Pour the batter into the prepared pan. Rotate the pan, evenly distributing the batter around the sides of the pan. Carefully sprinkle on the pine nuts.

4. Bake for 30 to 35 minutes, or until the top is golden brown; remove from oven and allow to cool for 1 hour. Carefully cut cake into diamond shapes.

5. Remove to a serving dish and serve at room temperature with tea!

Conclusion

I hope you enjoy these recipes as much as I've enjoyed creating and sharing them with you! Lebanese food is hearty, warm and filling and those are the ideals behind this book. So go ahead, try your hand out at these Lebanese favorites that are guaranteed to please!

Author's Afterthoughts

Thanks Ever So Much to Each of My Cherished Readers for Investing the Time to Read This Book!

I know you could have picked from many other books but you chose this one. So, big thanks for buying this book and reading all the way to the end.

If you enjoyed this book or received value from it, I'd like to ask you for a favor.

Printed in Great Britain
by Amazon

73463734R00047